T0208034

A Ninety-Day Empowerment Journal for Young Women

A Ninety-Day Empowerment Journal for Young Women

Learn to Affirm Daily Self-Love, Self-Confidence, and Self-Brilliance

Gwendolyn J. Cooke, PhD

A Ninety-Day Empowerment Journal for Young Women
Learn to Affirm Daily Self-Love, Self-Confidence, and Self-Brilliance

Scripture quotations marked KJV are from the Holy Bible, King James Version (Authorized Version). First published in 1611. Quoted from the KJV Classic Reference Bible, Copyright © 1983 by The Zondervan Corporation.

iUniverse books may be ordered through booksellers or by contacting:

iUniverse
1663 Liberty Drive
Bloomington, IN 47403
www.iuniverse.com
1-800-Authors (1-800-288-4677)

ISBN: 978-1-4917-6835-8 (sc)
ISBN: 978-1-4917-6837-2 (hc)
ISBN: 978-1-4917-6836-5 (e)

Library of Congress Control Number: 2015908361

Print information available on the last page.

iUniverse rev. date: 06/27/2015

To My Parents and My Teachers

To my parents and teachers who taught me
To be peaceful, loving, generous,
Grateful and thoughtful of others' needs.
Indeed, I have been blessed with the ability to see the glass
As "half-full" in the midst of tremendous
odds. That lesson alone
Compels me to "lift others as I continue to climb."

Much is required

Mentors continue to teach me that:

"Whoever has been given much will be responsible for much. Much more will be expected from the one who has been given more." Luke 12:47 (KJV)

To adolescent young women

Additionally, this journal is dedicated to adolescent young women who *are courageous* enough to commit to using this journal for *90 consecutive days*. As you write, be encouraged to use *the affirmation below* to sustain you on your journey to defining your future.

A Daily Affirmation for Success

I love myself, and I am worthy of others' love.
I am smart. I excel in and out of school daily.

For positive reinforcement of my beliefs about myself,
I will read daily
a poem by Langston Hughes or a poem by Maya Angelou.
As a teenage girl using this journal,
the world can become my creation when I
imagine it, write it, visualize it, plan it,
execute it, do it, and implement it!

I will preserve a right mental attitude.
This includes an attitude of courage,
frankness, and good cheer.
To think rightly is to create.

All things come through desire, and
every sincere prayer is answered.
Indeed, we become like that on which our hearts are fixed.

Contents

Foreword

Diana Daniels, Executive Director
National Council for Educating Black Children

What happens to a dream deferred? In *A Ninety-Day Empowerment Journal for Young Women*, the author, Dr. Gwendolyn J. Cooke, provides a blueprint for continuous attention to varied challenges that are unique to adolescent girls' maturation. In three parts—"Love Yourself," "Create Positive Relationships," and "You and Your Future"—adolescent girls are required to think and use a variety of resources to address successfully daily challenges they are experiencing. The attainment of dreams becomes more possible as they learn how to remain focused on their dreams and not have to defer achieving them because of poor decision making.

For example, take teenage girls' obsession with multimedia presentations of what is beautiful. Being thin is in. Showing skin is in. Short and tight—spandex preferably—is the cover of choice, and wearing it makes one all right. A face with lots of makeup trumps a light blush and lip gloss. Fashionable high-heeled shoes (that lead to feet problems for the rest of their lives) are a must!

Using a journal format, the author gains and maintains the interest of girls by using an "on spot" strategy. Entries into a journal are required. However, the required writing is not too long, nor is it too brief. Writing requirements are linked, moreover, to the Internet, a tool that students are required to use in most schools. Thus, the girls' skill with using technology is not viewed as only accessing "dull" work to be completed for their teachers. Many accessed sites will compel students to interact with parents, teachers, mentors, and peers. And boy, will they have fun!

This book "tells it like it is." Girls completing journal activities will gain understanding of the US Centers for Disease Control's six risk behaviors for teens:

1. Tobacco use
2. Unhealthy dietary behaviors
3. Inadequate physical activity
4. Alcohol and other drug use
5. Sexual behaviors that can result in HIV infection, other sexually transmitted diseases, and unintended pregnancies
6. Behaviors that may result in intentional injuries (such as violence and suicide) and unintentional injuries

What better place to discuss these issues than with a caring mentor and peers who have questions too? Journal writing is an appropriate strategy for problem solving when "talking it out" with a friend, parent, or another significant adult is not possible. It also fosters caution and further consultation with a trusted person before making important decisions.

If this book is gifted to a teen who does not have the opportunity to be a member of a group, it is highly recommended that the gift giver purchase two copies of the journal—one for the youth and one for the gift giver—so that the two of them may discuss the lessons as the adolescent girl finishes them. Dialogue with another person will increase the learning curve, and the harvest reaped will be great! Moreover, it will increase the possibility that the journal is used in keeping with how it was designed to be used.

There is a great need for this journal. Too many families are broken for many different reasons. Moreover, when girls need the "listening ears" of parents, foster parents, or a special teacher, too frequently those adults are not "present" to hear the cry for assistance, because the cry manifests itself in a hostile way. Having a journal to record thoughts and feelings is an excellent way to meet this need.

In conclusion, this book is an excellent example of a family involvement strategy advocated in the National Council on Educating Black Children (NCEBC) "Blueprint for Action" section that focuses on parents as stakeholders, leading and supporting their children from the cradle to adulthood.

Preface

I became an educator to help all students to achieve academically at the highest level. Even though I am now retired, my vision remains to assist young people to become all they can imagine and beyond. Academic performance is the standard measure of achievement by local, state and national institutions, and this remains important. However, as I reflected about young women's needs, I concluded that social success is just as important as academic attainment.

As a teacher, an administrator and as superintendent, I experienced first-hand how too many brilliant teenage females engaged in inappropriate social behavior. It broke my heart to see teen girls make unwise and far reaching choices. For example, two beautiful, intelligent young ladies, who were both pregnant by the same boy, get into a fight in their science class. The young man was the general and the specific reasons for the fight. These 16 year olds literally destroyed the classroom and faced expulsion from school. These two young ladies' whose life had already been irrevocably altered --- by the decisions they made that resulted in each of them becoming pregnant. Now, they placed in jeopardy their opportunity to complete their high school education; I wondered why these young women would choose a few thrills with a 16 year old boy verses a bright future.

Poor decision making is not an isolated event. The circumstances may be different, but similar outcomes are seen daily in schools across our great country. Beautiful, intelligent young women make thoughtless, rash choices that result in the use of drugs and/or alcohol, bullying, negative peer pressure, dropping out of school, self-doubt, and despair. Each young woman needs a mentor and carefully designed and structured activities to help her excel and successfully manage her own future.

A Ninety-Day Empowerment Journal for Young Women is a guide for teenagers and young women ages thirteen to twenty-one, including college students. It is intended to be read with an adult mentor who will work with a group of peers to ensure adequate coverage of the topic for maximum benefit. However, this book can also be used by an individual young woman who wants to grow and develop on her own.

Use of Common Core Standards, Depth of Knowledge, and Multiple Intelligences

As a life-long educator, I embrace the Common Core standards and Webb's Depth of Knowledge, which academically prepare students to be successful in college and/or careers. The learning activities in this journal are designed to address standards for English Language Arts/Literacy and Speaking and Listening. For more information on Depth of Knowledge, view the video at https://www.youtube.com/watch?v=WMqKN7edRcU.

The resources and activities throughout the book are consistent with Common Core and Depth of Knowledge. The journal requires users to think strategically and extend their thinking—to reason, investigate a set of conditions, make judgments and choices, and develop and monitor a plan. It will also facilitate the development of a young woman's unique voice and build her sense of empowerment, confidence, and self-esteem. It is hoped that each reader is inspired to love herself and others more and to make a plan that ensures fulfillment of the biggest dreams she has for herself.

"Multiple intelligences" are the nine intelligences through which students learn:

1. Verbal-linguistic (reading, listening, speaking, writing)
2. Mathematical-logical (reasoning and problem solving, numbers)
3. Musical (songs, patterns, rhythms, instruments, musical expression)
4. Visual-spatial (thinking in images and pictures, seeing things in one's mind)
5. Bodily/kinesthetic (interaction with one's environment, concrete experiences)
6. Intrapersonal (feelings, values, and attitudes; understanding other people)
7. Interpersonal (interactions with others, working collaboratively and cooperatively)
8. Naturalist (classification, categories, and hierarchies; ability to pick up on subtle differences)
9. Existential (seeing the big picture, connecting real-world learning and application to new learning

An Intervention Tool for Varied Users

The audience for this book is vast. Young women attending traditional schools, those in after-school or weekend programs, and those in specialized settings—as well as the adults who serve them as mentors, teachers, social workers, and guidance counselors—are in great need of the content presented here. Young women desperately need to have hope, to understand the value of education, and to seek the rewards of empowerment. Settings in which the book might be used include the following:

- Boys and Girls Clubs
- character-education programs and/or intervention programs
- health classes
- in-school suspension

- homeroom classes (if divided by gender)
- independent study
- teenage-pregnancy classes
- juvenile-justice classes
- foster-care groups
- homeless centers
- Girl Scouts
- church ministries
- sororities and fraternities
- science/physical-education classes
- after-school programs

It is expected that many mentors will accept the call of adolescents and young adults who need positive role models. Essentially, every sorority, association, club, civic group, social group, and church group cares deeply about the future of black teens and young adult females. Countless numbers of these local, state, and national organizations have a youth program in place. These groups need programs that are easy to deliver, well planned, and certain to have a positive impact on the females whom they serve. *A Ninety-Day Empowerment Journal for Young Women* is one tool for which volunteer groups have been searching.

Introduction

A Ninety-Day Empowerment Journal is a guide for girls and young women who are influenced by the negative images presented in various media of African American youth and young adults. These images usually question the youths' values and the overarching influence of poverty on their behavior. This book will provide positive sustaining strategies and boosts to self-esteem for young females who may not see themselves as achievers—socially, emotionally, and/or economically.

In this introduction, there are specific messages for the adult mentors and for the teens and young women who will be using this journal.

For Adult Mentors

This book is intended to be used with an adult mentor who will work with—support, cajole, encourage, push, and humor—teenage users of this book. *A Ninety-Day Empowerment Journal for Young Women* provides activities and resources that reinforce important outcomes: meeting Common Core standards, learning Depth of Knowledge, and developing into sensitive, problem-solving adults.

Mentoring

Group leaders who facilitate discussions will serve as accessible, caring, kind, loving, affirming mentors and role models. Mentors will demonstrate these values through their positive attitude, self-determined disposition, tone of voice, openness, honesty, warm style, and positive acceptance of the ideas of their mentees. Mentors are guided to facilitate discussions as described in the journal. They are also encouraged to use the recommended resources for each activity. These activities use various intelligences to increase the likelihood of student success and engagement.

Through the planned reflective journaling process, those female adults who choose to be mentors will remain extremely important because both the mentor and the mentee are positively impacted in the following ways:

- Mentors want to make a difference in their own lives by helping to make a difference in the lives of female adolescents and young adults.
- Adolescents and young adults need to know there are adults who care about them, in addition to their parents.
- Mentors will share their life experiences with adolescents and young adults so that these students will not have to repeat the mistakes their mentors have made.
- Adolescents will build relationships with positive female role models they can emulate, in addition to family members, teachers, and those in their immediate circle.
- Mentors will help adolescents and young adults learn the art and science of positive affirmations, the process used to think through and solve problems, and moving forward decisively with confidence.
- Adolescents and young adults will affirm their mentors and the mentors will affirm them, thereby replacing any negative self-talk with care, understanding, goal-setting, and positive forward momentum.
- Mentors will in turn expect that, even while the young females are being mentored, they will in turn choose a younger girl to mentor. As it should be in the world we are creating, no matter where we are in life and no matter what we are doing, we must have time to share

what we have learned with those still arriving where we have passed. In this duality of lifelong mentorship, mentoring while we are being mentored (giving and receiving), teen and young adult mentors will receive personal gratification and learn more about themselves.

Use of the Internet

The Internet is central to making effective use of this journal, as references to specific videos and content are linked to the activities. The sites not only add significant content for users to think about, but they are often enjoyable and add to the user's level of knowledge. Please note that the content available on any Internet site is subject to change. Consequently, the specific link for the information referred to in the activities may have changed between the time of this writing and the time the user needs to access the required information. If this happens, do not worry. There is a constant regeneration of information available on the Internet. Simply type in the keywords used in the specific activity to locate similar information.

Access to a Computer

A computer is required to complete many of the assignments. If a teenager or young woman does not have a personal computer, she can access one at no cost at most public libraries, schools, churches, Boys and Girls Clubs, or other organizations that have after-school programs for young people. If a teenager is still unable to locate a computer, mentors are requested to assist in this task.

Facilitation Instructions

Predictable routines are as effective as you make them. Therefore, it is recommended that mentors adhere to these three points as they facilitate the girls' use of this journal:

- Read aloud daily the directions for which the activities have been designed.
- Respond daily to specific questions that address issues in the activities either verbally, in writing, in artwork, or using other intelligences.
- Insist daily that students engage in deeper reflection with fellow users in small groups.

Mentors should review the following section, aimed at teenagers and young adult women, for more important information.

Teenagers and Young Adults

Congratulations! You have made a wise choice by selecting this journal to use for your personal growth and development. As a teen or a young adult, you have probably already noticed that few people know "you are the queen you are." But that is okay, because life is full of surprises for all of us. What is important is that you begin to intentionally "accentuate the positive and eliminate the negative" from your life. When you hold a copy of this journal in your hands, your behavior says that you are open to new knowledge and positive experiences. Great!

Do you know that it takes at least twenty-one consecutive days to form a new habit? Continuing most tasks for twenty-one consecutive days is difficult. However, since you have acquired this guide and are using it to improve some aspect of your life, your determination to use it for ninety consecutive days is a message to yourself that "I know I can!"

Lessons in this Journal

A commitment to believing in yourself and developing the daily habit of taking twenty minutes of quiet time to think, dream, and write about your challenges is a proven strategy for success. These or similar habits that involve "practice, practice, practice" have served adolescent athletes, accomplished young singers, dancers, actors, preachers, and others who remain at the top of their game. Therefore, you are encouraged to revisit the journal exercises in this book more than once. Challenges will continue to visit you throughout adulthood. Confronting challenges is part of being alive and human, so contemplation and trial and error are critical to success.

It is okay not to complete all tasks correctly the first time; repeated visits to tasks not fully completed can lead to better outcomes. You are encouraged to revisit the last three entry and reflection sections of this guide. Your continuous success depends upon this habit of mind and practice.

Journal Entries and Reflections

A conscious effort has been made to motivate you to use this journal to complete activities, followed by group participation with three or more female peers. The synergy and benefits resulting from group interactions increase the probability that you will act on the learning and skills developed from such connections. Thus, herein we focus on action for personal growth and responsibility, the sought-after outcomes.

Writing a Daily Journal

A journal is a record with entries arranged by date reporting on what has happened over the course of a day or some other period. A personal journal includes the experiences, thoughts, and feelings of the person writing the journal, including comments on current events.

Although you will write answers to questions in this journal, such entries will be insufficient to record all your thoughts and ideas. Use of the Internet will also impact on your journaling, because of the format of some documents. Therefore, you will need to purchase or create a binder with about a hundred pages. Daily entries will vary depending on the experiences you are having. One word on a piece of paper might be sufficient for one journal entry. However, several sentences of at least three paragraphs will require you to be increasingly more reflective about the experiences you are having as you move into womanhood.

It is recommended that you make it a habit to write in your journal daily. The activities will help you with daily writing, because you may want to record your reaction to a specific action that you have completed for group discussion.

The Ninety-Day Challenge

Along with completing the activities in this guide for the next ninety days, you will maintain a journal that will include entries related to the assigned activities and entries related to gratitude. The following activities offer you an opportunity to visualize:

- Think about and write about how each day is going or has been, what's going well, and what is within your power to change.
- Sit quietly. Reflect, and get in touch with those internal thoughts and feelings you have perhaps never noticed but have been lingering beneath the surface, waiting to positively influence you and your future.
- As you write in your journal, you will use two to three pages to respond to questions asked. The last three pages of your journal should be labeled "Gratitude Journal." In

this section, you will write statements that reflect your grateful spirit—what you value and are happy to have. It will not always be a person, place, or thing. It can also be, for example, pride in what you have accomplished, a calm life, a happy experience, or a giving heart.

- Visualize positive outcomes that you can see in your mind's eye for yourself, the people you love, and those who love you. To visualize, close your eyes for six or seven minutes and breathe in and out slowly to clear your mind of all thoughts.

- Engage in meaningful discussion with your adult mentor and several other females in a small group. Your group's goal is to complete each of the activities in this journal so that you can unlock your potential to succeed beyond your current expectations.

Your experiences have a visual component. Whatever you experience now is the result of what you have consciously or unconsciously visualized. Visualization is based on the recognition that your mind is open, and that in fact you are creating your own reality all the time. Visualization is a creative cognitive activity; it is not daydreaming. It is accessible to any thinking person. For adolescent girls and young women to realize that this life-validating strategy is available to achieve goals is powerful. Throughout this journal, you will be encouraged to visualize various positive outcomes.

When you are negative, fearful, insecure, or anxious, you tend to attract the very experiences, situations, or people you are seeking to avoid. On the other hand, if you are normally positive in attitude—expecting and envisioning simple pleasures, satisfaction, and happiness—you will tend to attract people and create situations and events which meet your positive expectations. So the more positive energy you put into visualizing what you want, the more it begins to manifest in your life.

What is important for users of this journal to understand is that when you approach problem solving in a proactive rather than a passive way, you increase the likelihood of success. Your goals may be on any level—physical, emotional, mental, or spiritual. You may, for example, imagine yourself with a cell phone with all the bells and whistles; a wardrobe that your peers envy; a beautiful, loving, and fulfilling relationship; a feeling of calm and serenity; or perhaps an improved memory and learning ability. You might picture yourself handling a difficult situation effortlessly, or simply see yourself as a radiant being, filled with light and love. You may work on any level, and all will have results. Through experience, you will find the particular images and techniques which work best for you. The exercises in this journal provide practice opportunities in a safe and affirming environment under the supervision of a mentor.

A Gratitude Journal

As mentioned earlier in this section, along with visualization experiences, there is the opportunity for you to keep a gratitude journal. The author of this book define *gratitude* as the most passionate transformative force in the cosmos. By using a gratitude journal in addition to *A Ninety-Day Empowerment Journal for Young Women*, you will learn that you already possess everything you need to be genuinely happy. All you truly need is the grateful awareness of all that you have.

Some days, writing about gratitude will be easy. Other days, the only thing you might be thankful for is that the day is over. A mutually affirming relationship with your mentor will sustain both of you.

Affirmations

An affirmation is a mental or verbal declaration to yourself and to the universe about how you want your life to be. Words and thoughts are powerful. Too often, females fail to identify their tremendous abilities and intellect as well as their inner beauty and numerous positive personal traits.

Affirmations can assist each teen and young woman in perceiving herself as a brilliant achiever. In part 1, "Love Yourself," you will be asked in exercises 1.3 and 1.4 to write affirmations for at least ten days. It is hoped that you will find these affirmations as powerful in your life as they have been in the life of the author of this book.

Journal Format

A Ninety-Day Empowerment Journal for Young Women is separated into three parts, each with fifteen to sixteen exercises.

- Part 1: Love Yourself
- Part 2: Create Positive Relationships
- Part 3: You and Your Future

Part 1

Love Yourself

This section includes the following exercises:

1.1 Isn't She Lovely?

Access the Stevie Wonder song "Isn't She Lovely?" at http://www.youtube.com/watch?v=IVvkjuEAwgU. Listen to the song and view the lyrics. Then, using the letters of LOVELY, write a meaning for each letter to describe what is LOVELY about you. The words given here are examples; please choose different words.

L   Likable _____
O   Outstanding _____
V   Vivacious _____
E   Enthusiastic _____
L   Lively _____
Y   Young at heart _____

Now create a collage of words and pictures depicting how you feel about yourself at this moment. Choose a person with whom to share your collage. How did she feel? What did you learn?

1.2 Encouragement

Read the poems "Mother to Son" by Langston Hughes and "Still I Rise" by Maya Angelou, available at http://www. poemhunter.com/poem/still-i-rise/. Listen to Maya Angelou recite her poem on YouTube at https://www.youtube.com/watch?v=vXCHKWFmU2s. Listen to the recitation of "Mother to Son" by a female reader and the poet, Langston Hughes, at https://www.youtube.com/watch?v=NX9tHuI7zVo.

Explain below how encouragement is defined in each poem. Explain the specific message of each poem.

Poem	"Mother to Son"	"Still I Rise"
Define encouragement		
Poem's message		

With a partner, discuss how these poems are alike and how they're different. How did these poems encourage you? Write your own poem about encouragement in your journal. Audiotape or videotape your performance.

1.3 Journal-Writing Introduction

Access the web page at http://dayoneapp.com/journal-series/what-to-journal/ to respond to the following question about journaling. To learn more about journaling, click on the other articles in the series of four.

What is a journal?

_____

_____

Give three reasons why the author or others chose to journal.

    1. _____

    2. _____

    3. _____

Give two reasons why you could journal.

    1. _____

    2. _____

Below the poem you wrote about encouragement in your journal in exercise 1.2, write your second journal entry, and copy it below.

Be prepared to discuss your journal entry with a group member at the next session.

1.4 Journal Writing

There is some truth to the expression "that which we practice is usually what we excel in." To increase your success with setting goals and achieving them, it is recommended that you begin keeping a journal and that you write in the journal daily. The journal does not have to be a fancy document that you want to show your best friend and brag about. The journal is a tool that will contribute to your self-reflection and success with goals and objectives that you identify.

Every day for ninety days, write in your journal. Some sample sentences are provided for you to start with. You are to write each sentence ten times. The second week, you are to identify affirmations and other words you would like to write and think about. A list of affirmations appears in the appendix should you find it difficult to identify sentences and expressions to use.

Most people will agree that habits may be considered good or bad. In reality, a habit is simply a behavior acquired by frequent repetition. The author of this book wants you to practice behavior that will become a habit. Sit quietly and write in your journal for fifteen minutes daily. Sitting silently and writing (a form of meditation) becomes your private time to reflect and think about what is important to you and make both long- and short-range plans. Follow these steps to get the most out of your fifteen minutes of journal-writing time:

1. Read the affirmation silently.
2. Read the affirmation aloud five to ten times.
3. Write the affirmation in your journal ten times.
4. After you have done this, skip a line on your paper and write these words: "I am grateful that I am remaining focused on using my journal daily."

Complete your writing by expressing gratitude about the growth that is taking place in your life.

After the first six days of writing affirmations and expressing gratitude, identify one to three goals that you would like to accomplish in the next three weeks. Your mentor (the person assisting you with using this book) will model possible responses for you and give more details.

Daily Affirmations

Monday

Success in life is not a mystery. Commitment and hard work are the keys to achieving my dreams.

Tuesday

I will discard negative thoughts. I will accentuate the positive in myself and others.

Wednesday

Happiness is contagious. I will share my smile and words of praise.

Thursday

Remember—it is the little things that mean so much. Good relationships are based on respect, communication, and consideration. I communicate clearly and politely. I am considerate of others' needs.

Friday

Adapting to change is the secret to survival. I will stay flexible and not worry about nonsense or about the small stuff.

Reread periodically the sentences that you have written down. When you do, you will increase the tasks and goals that you have identified for yourself.

Sample Goals

1. I will complete my homework nightly before I watch TV or play any electronic games.

2. I will say thank you with a smile to my family, friends, and teachers when they are kind to me.
3. I will write my priorities, tasks, and a list with action steps to identify the alternatives I have to respond to specific situations.
4. I will maximize my dietary profits by doing the following:
   - cutting down on total fat intake
   - eating more high-fiber foods
   - choosing fruits and vegetables for snacks
   - drinking six to eight glasses of water a day

Looking Ahead

Soon, your journal will not be limited to copying or writing goals and affirmations. You might be writing questions to help you problem-solve and/or raise your spirits. As you write in your journal, notice how many of your thoughts are positive and how many are negative. Which types of statements will guide you toward being creative, thoughtful, and optimistic about the concern at hand?

Believe in yourself. Keep your mind on your dream. Discuss with your mentor how to set goals.

1.5 Proud to Be Female

There are many challenges that females face daily. Read "10 Challenges That American Women Still Face Today" on the *Ms. Magazine* site at http://msmagazine.com/blog/2013/05/31/10-challenges-that-american-women-still-face-today/. List three challenges that you face now or are likely to experience in the future.

1.
2.
3.

Even though females face barriers, quickly list six things that are positive about being female:

1.
2.
3.
4.
5.
6.

Friends

Using your journal, poll five peers to determine how many of the items on their lists are the same as yours. Now focus on the beautiful things about being female that your peers listed but you did not. What surprised you about the items you didn't list? Has your impression of being a young woman changed as a result of this activity? If yes, why? If no, why not?

1.6 Loving Yourself

How you feel about who you are is determined by your level of self-esteem and self-confidence. Your self-esteem or self-regard is comprised of how you feel about your traits or qualities, both internal and external. Your internal traits are your private feelings, values, thoughts, and actions, whether about yourself or about your relationships with others. Your external traits are the obvious physical qualities that you and others can readily see, such as your height, weight, and the color of your eyes. It is natural to feel higher or lower levels of self-esteem in new and different situations. Use the chart below to list five of your external traits and five of your internal traits.

External Traits	Internal Traits

How do you feel about your external traits? How do you feel about your internal traits? How do you feel about your combined external and internal traits?

1.7 You Are Unique

There is no one else like you anywhere in the world. Embrace your uniqueness. What makes you unique in each of these different settings?

- Home _____
- School _____
- Church _____
- With friends _____
- Hanging out _____
- Participating in organized sports or activities

_____

The combination of these different settings and your own uniqueness are what makes you who you are. Below, write a paragraph about who you are. Rewrite your answer in your journal.

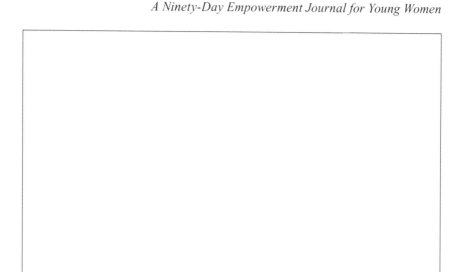

1.8 Respect Yourself

Listen to "Respect" sung by Aretha Franklin, available on YouTube at http://www.youtube.com/watch?v=6FOUqQt3Kg0&feature=kp. Then listen to "I Will Survive" sung by Gloria Gaynor at http://www.youtube.com/watch?v=Tth-8wA3PdY. After listening to both songs, write down the message that each song gives to women.

• "Respect":

• "I Will Survive":

Women have choices. You can choose to demonstrate that you truly respect and love all aspects of yourself. Use your suggestions and those of three peers to identify specific actions you will choose to take to demonstrate that you truly love and respect yourself and others. Write them here.

- I will love and respect my body by:

- I will love and respect my mind by:

- I will love and respect my peers by:

- I will love and respect my heritage by:

Write what you learned most about love and respect as a result of this activity.

1.9 Interacting with Others

Form a group of up to four of your friends to discuss the question, "What do you think about students who make good grades?" Go deeper to find out why you or they may have been teased for making good grades. Ask one another "why" three times in the following way:

1. Ask, "Why would a person be teased for making good grades?"
2. Given the answer to number one, ask, "Why is that?"
3. Given the answer to number two, ask, "Why is that?"

If you're someone who teases your peers for making good grades, go deeper with that as well. Ask one another "why" three times:

1. Ask, "Why would you tease a peer for making good grades?"
2. Given the answer to number one, ask, "Why is that?"
3. Given the answer to number two, ask, "Why is that?"

Role-play how you will respond the next time someone teases you about being smart. Now role-play the part of the teaser. After the role-play, share your insight with the larger group. Write below what you learned as a result of this process. Rewrite your answer in your journal.

1.10 Where Do You Draw the Line?

Young ladies must be very careful not to abandon their morals and values for money. After reading the short article "Difference between Morals and Values" on the DiffenceBetween.info site at http://www.differencebetween.info/difference-between-morals-and-values, write your definition of morals and values.

- Morals are:
- Values are:

Now complete the following:

"I am clear and firm; I will not give up the following morals or values for temporary success, for any job in my future or for any female or male."

1.
2.
3.

Your mentor will lead the group in a discussion about everyone's responses to this question. As each participant responds, your mentor will publically tally the results. Be prepared to share your answers.

1.11 Beauty Is More Than Skin Deep

Beauty comes in all colors, sizes, and shapes, yet our view of beauty too often fits into a little box based on what the media has told us is beautiful. Read "What Is Beauty and Who Has It?" by Arlene Dawson on the CNN website at http://www.cnn.com/2011/LIVING/06/29/global.beauty.culture/ and then explain what you learned about beauty in America.

I learned ...

Look into a mirror, smile, and say out loud this affirmation: "I am beautiful." Keep smiling as you repeat this affirmation nine times. Now write down how you feel about yourself after the tenth time.

I feel ...

Confer with three peers to share how you each feel about this activity. Write what you learned from this activity below. Rewrite your answer in your journal.

I learned …

Repeat this activity every day before you leave home: Look in the mirror, smile, and say to yourself, "I am beautiful." Do it every day until you really believe it. Then keep doing it to ensure that you continue to believe it.

1.12 Feeling Down?

It is perfectly normal to feel down sometimes. Everyone feels this way at times, regardless of age, gender, income, position, or location. The question is, what can you do to bring back your happiness during these periods of time? Access the "Feeling Happy" index page on the GirlsHealth.gov site at http://www. girlshealth.gov/feelings/happy/index.html. Read the sections linked in pink in the upper left corner, and click on the links within those sections. Share what you learned below.

Self-esteem is:

Three strategies I plan to use to boost my self-esteem are:

  1.
  2.
  3.

Self-confidence is:

Three strategies I plan to use to boost my self-confidence are:

  1.
  2.
  3.

Confer with a member of the group to compare and contrast your responses. Describe below how you feel about "feeling down sometimes" after completing this activity.

1.13 Images of Girls and Women of Color

When you look in the mirror, what do you see? You must see the very beautiful you! Surf the web to find pictures of at least ten beautiful girls and women of color. Print these pictures and use them to create a collage of beautiful ladies. To make your collection really beautiful, include pictures of girls and ladies of several different ages and various shades of color.

Display your collage with each member of the group's collage for viewing by all. Compare and contrast your collages below and then share your responses. What did you learn about the beauty of women of color, and what did you learn about your own beauty?

- Women of color:

- My own beauty:

1.14 Your High Self-Esteem

High self-esteem or positive internal thoughts and feelings let you know that you have many resources. You are not helpless. You are as equal, valuable, creditable, smart, and worthwhile as others. Your self-esteem assures you that you have the power to make good decisions that will positively influence you for the rest of your life. It also helps you to know that you are not superior to anyone and no one is superior to you.

Throughout life, you will have to train your internal voice to feed you positive information about yourself in messages like this:

A misstep is a temporary setback, but you will pick yourself up, brush yourself off, and proceed to succeed in life. You will reach your goals; you will graduate from high school and go on to graduate from college. You are a compassionate, caring, giving, and genuinely kind person who readily helps others and never takes advantage. You treat people like you want to be treated.

Read the article "Three Steps to Improved Self-Esteem" on the University of Texas site at http://cmhc.utexas.edu/selfesteem.html#8 and then write your answers to the following questions about self-esteem:

1. What is self-esteem?
2. What is the difference between poor and healthy self-esteem?
3. Where does self-esteem come from?
4. What does your inner voice say?
5. What are the three faces of low self-esteem?
6. What are the consequences of low self-esteem?
7. What are three steps you can use to improve your self-esteem?

In the space below, explain what you will do to continue to build your self-esteem:

Be prepared to share your responses with the mentoring group. Rewrite your response in your journal.

1.15 Weight Management: A Daily Activity

Surely you, like most teens and young adults, want to look your very best every day. Teens and adults who are naturally thin are that way because they have, perhaps unknowingly, incorporated great eating and exercise habits into their everyday lives.

Access the article "Take Charge of Your Health: A Guide for Teenagers" on the US Department of Health and Human Services site at http://www.niddk.nih.gov/health-information/health-topics/weight-control/take-charge-your-health/Pages/take-charge-your-health.aspx. Read the five sections. For each of the sections, write what you are currently doing and what the article suggests that you do:

Know How Your Body Works

I am currently:	It's suggested that I:

Charge Up with Healthy Eating

I am currently:	It's suggested that I:

Get Moving

I am currently:	It's suggested that I:

Take Your Time

I am currently:	It's suggested that I:

Make It Work for You

I am currently:	It's suggested that I:

Identify five friends, family members, or others who look great. Ask them about their eating habits and exercise habits. Record their responses below.

Name and Age	Eating Habits	Exercise Habits

Below, explain how closely their eating and exercise habits reflect the advice suggested in your research.

Given what you are doing and what you have learned, make a seven-day plan for how you will change your eating habits and/ or your exercise habits to be mentally and physically healthier, more fit, and able to look and feel your best.

Day of the Week	New Eating Habits	New Exercise Habits
Monday		
Tuesday		
Wednesday		
Thursday		
Friday		
Saturday		
Sunday		

Choose a friend to serve as a buddy, and keep each other on track. Compare notes, and continue to make this plan a routine.

1.16 How Do Girls Attract Boys?

Some teenage girls go to great lengths to attract boys. Yet despite all they do, their efforts may have the opposite effect. Rather than attracting boys, their appearances and behaviors may in fact be turnoffs. Boys may either run away or have a short fling with a girl and leave her feeling brokenhearted and more desperate to attract a boy than ever. The following are some of the ways girls try too hard to attract boys:

- pretend to be people other than who they are
- wear too much makeup

- starve themselves to get what they perceive to be the "perfect body"
- pretend not to be smart
- drink alcohol, smoke, and/or take drugs
- be sexually permissive
- tell lies
- wear low-cut tops and very short and tight skirts

On the other hand, here are several ways girls may consider to attract boys they would really like to get to know:

- simply be themselves
- wear just enough makeup to highlight their natural features
- show their sense of humor
- smile
- be smart and capable
- be independent (self-disciplined)
- be neat, clean, and healthy
- be physically fit

Think about each of the items listed above. Circle those that you disagree with, and write a statement beside the item expressing why you believe this is not true.

Now make ten copies of the following survey to distribute to male students. Select ten boys to ask if they agree or disagree with each item on this survey. You may choose boys from your school, church, family, or other places you go.

Gwendolyn J. Cooke, PhD

Male Student Survey		Age:
Is a girl who behaves as described below trying too hard to attract boys?	**Yes**	**No**
pretends to be someone other than who she is		
wears too much makeup		
starves herself to get what she thinks is the "perfect body"		
pretends not to be smart		
drinks alcohol, smokes, and/or takes drugs		
is sexually permissive		
lies		
wears short and tight clothes		
Will a girl who behaves as described below attract boys?	**Yes**	**No**
is comfortable simply being herself		
wears just enough makeup to highlight her natural features		
shows you her sense of humor		
smiles often		
is smart and capable		
is independent and self-disciplined		
is neat, clean, and healthy		
is physically fit		

Source: http://www.teennewz.com/gallery/7021/crazy-things-girls-do-to-attract-guys/74940.

After you have collected the ten surveys, total the number who agree and the number who disagree with each item on the list.

Awareness Tips

- Take note of the information you get from the boys. Their opinions are important.
- The boys you interview may attempt to change the topic under discussion. They may also answer your questions by asking you a question; for example, "What do you think? Don't you agree with me?"
- The boys may want you to share your opinion about specific people the two of you know. They will use their mothers as an example and link your mother's behavior to their answers.
- The boys may be evasive and profess that they are not going to answer or comment on some of your questions.
- You will need to appeal to the better self of each male peer. Indicate that you really need his cooperation, because your success with the group that you are a member of depends on his thoughts, so that relationships between teenage boys and girls can be reciprocal and respectful.

Change the topic under discussion if necessary. Repeatedly ask a question that is not clear until the boy responding to your survey understands.

Below, write a summary statement of the boys' responses. Include the ages of the boys you surveyed. Was there a difference in the response of the boys of different ages? For example, "Fourteen-year-old boys believed ..."

Behaviors seen as "trying too hard":
Behaviors that really do attract boys:

For the final step, visually depict "trying too hard" and "behaviors that will attract boys" by surfing the web to locate pictures of stars or others with too much makeup and too-revealing clothes and those with "less is more" makeup and clothing. Save pictures in each category in your electronic photo gallery to share with your mentoring group.

Part 2

Create Positive Relationships

This section includes the following exercises:

2.1 Parents: Your First and Lasting Teachers

Approximately 49 percent of children are being raised by a single parent—a mother, a father, a grandparent or other relative, or a foster parent. Thus, it becomes important that young people establish healthy, productive relationships with whoever assumes the role of parent. There are many examples of successful people who were raised by one parent or one adult who cared about them; for example, President Barack Obama, Angelina Jolie, Halle Berry, Maya Angelou, and former President Bill Clinton. Everyone's family is different.

Describe your family situation and the relationships between you, your mother and father, and the other children, if you have brothers or sisters. Are your parents living together or living apart? Is the relationship warm, loving and welcoming? What other words would you use to describe your family?

It is generally understood that parents are just people who are trying to do the best they can with what they have been given. Do you agree with this statement? Why or why not? Think about the concept of forgiving people for their mistakes. Do you think it's important to be able to forgive people? How will forgiving others benefit you? Write your answers below.

I agree or disagree with the statement because

I think it is important/not important to forgive people because

Forgiving others can benefit me by

2.2 Models for Problem Solving

Think about people who have achieved in spite of extreme hardships. Many have made exceptional achievements in their fields in spite of severe obstacles. Individually, they have chosen to become inventors of their own lives. Reading and analyzing biographies can provide models for you. The stories can help you to solve problems and give you clues to steps you might take to reinvent your life.

Search the web for information on one of your favorite female stars. It can be an entertainer, actor, athlete, or anyone whose biography you are likely to find online. Read the biography and take notes to explain how this individual chose to become an inventor of her life. Using the form below, write your plan for how you will reinvent one aspect of your life.

What one or two things will you do, beginning tomorrow, to reinvent your own life? What will you add in the second and third weeks?

Steps to Reinvent My Life

Week 1

Week 2

Week 3

When you go home tonight, thank your mom, dad, and/ or others for one thing that you appreciate about them. Each time your mentoring group meets over the next three weeks, select a partner to share each other's weekly progress on steps to reinvent your life.

2.3 Conversations with Adults

Many teenagers find it difficult to carry on a conversation with adults. Some find it even more difficult to build positive relationships with adults. After reading "Talking to Your Parents— or Other Adults" on the KidsHealth site at http://kidshealth.org/teen/your_mind/families/talk_to_parents.html to learn why it's important to build positive relationships with adults and how you can approach it, complete the following exercise.

- Identify an adult with whom you would like to build a better relationship:

- Write how this relationship will benefit you:

- Write how this relationship will benefit the adult:

List three strategies you will use to begin the conversation.

1. One strategy is to identify what you have in common. List three commonalities:

   a.
   b.
   c.

2. Then list two other strategies:

   a.
   b.

You are encouraged to initiate a conversation with a parent or adult whenever you can. The above format will serve as a source for starting your conversations with the individual you identified. At the next group session, be prepared to share the success you had talking with the identified adult.

From your reading, list three new points to extend the conversation with your parent or other adult in the next week.

1.

2.

3.

2.4 Family History

"History, despite its wrenching pain, cannot be unlived,
but if faced with courage, need not be lived again."

"The love of the family, the love of one person
can heal. It heals the scars left by a larger
society. A massive, powerful society."

—Maya Angelou quotes from http://blog.sfgate.com/ hottopics/2014/05/28/10-inspiring-quotes-from-maya-angelou/

It is important and informative for you to know your family's history and your ethnic or racial history. Knowing your history can give you a stronger sense of connectedness to your living relatives, your ancestors (relatives who have passed away), and your own present identity. Collecting family stories of relatives is a great way to begin learning about your family history.

Choose a relative to interview—if possible, your oldest living relative would be best. Access two articles on About.com

Genealogy: "How to Interview a Relative" at http://genealogy. about.com/cs/oralhistory/ht/interview.htm and "Fifty Questions for Family History Interviews" at http://genealogy.about.com/ cs/oralhistory/a/interview.htm. Follow the directions in "How to Interview a Relative" to set up the interview, and then select twenty questions from the list of fifty that you find interesting to ask your relative. Write or type the questions out in advance, before the interview, and then add your relative's response to each question.

Bring your interview to the next mentoring session, and be prepared to share it with your group. Write below three pieces of new information that you found out about your family background as a result of this interview:

1.
2.
3.

Share with a partner first and then with the mentoring group how you felt learning this new information.

2.5 Frank Discussions about Sex

If you attend Sunday school and/or church regularly, over the course of several years it is highly possible that your minister and your parent/caregiver gave you similar messages about "responsible vs. irresponsible" sexual activity. Share with a partner the words your caregiver or minister used to describe irresponsible sexual activity. Be prepared to discuss your definitions with the group. What are the nonnegotiable points of *responsible* sexual activity? Why is it necessary for you to insist that the male with whom you are having sex wears a condom? Compare and contrast your responses below.

Abstinence	Irresponsible Sexual Activity	Responsible Sexual Activity

Which road will you choose to follow: abstinence, irresponsibility, or responsible sexual activity? Explain why you made this choice.

2.6 "No Means No!"

Both male and female teenagers change their minds a lot during adolescence, ages thirteen to eighteen. That's okay, because this is a time of tremendous change in your thinking skills and in the maturation of your body. As a female, your sexual organs (breasts) experience rapid growth and your skin is most sensitive to someone massaging or touching you lightly or "feeling on you"—breast, buttocks, arms, hands, etc. Such touching can lead to physical fistfights, name-calling, laughing, challenges to each other, crying, and similar behavior. This usually results in boys concluding that you act so "confusing." Therefore, it is most important that you speak clearly to boys about what kind of touching/words/teasing is okay and what is not. It becomes important that you

- ask questions;
- communicate clearly and firmly;
- understand what each of you wants; and
- understand if you are right for each other.

With a peer, make a list of at least five things that you find to be different and perhaps confusing about boys' behavior.

1.
2.
3.
4.
5.

Share your list with your mentoring group. Verbally note the similarities and differences among the lists presented.

Identify a responsible male and female in your life who can give you his-and-her perspectives on the male behaviors you find puzzling. Report back the results of your conversation with these adults at the next mentoring session.

2.7 Are Men and Women Really Different?

You and your mentoring group are not the only ones who think women and men are very different from one another. A very popular book titled *Men Are From Mars, Women Are From Venus* was written to acknowledge that the differences are so great it is like men and women come from different planets.

A synopsis of the book is available at http://www.slideshare. net/kayeaalejandro/john-gray-men-are-from-mars-women- are-from-venus. There are thirteen chapters in the book. Each chapter has been summarized to reveal the main idea for each chapter. Using the book summary as a guide, each member of the mentoring group is asked to select a different chapter to read and write out the main idea. Add whether you agree or disagree with what you read. Use evidence to support your position of agreement or disagreement.

Each member of the mentoring group will have an opportunity to report. Given all that has been reported and the feedback from the adult man and woman you interviewed, what possible explanations can you think of for the male behaviors that puzzle you? What did you learn from this exercise?

2.8 Social Media

Social media—including Facebook, Twitter, Instagram, and Tumblr—are among the best-known sites that teenagers frequent. These sites are valuable for staying in touch with friends and relatives; they are highly interactive and can be great fun. These services are commonly used to bring together people who are interested in the same topics; you can follow groups for your school, family, music, dance, science, mathematics, and so forth.

However, depending on the choices you make, these same social-media sites can be very damaging to you and to others. Why? Because what you write and post on the World Wide Web will always be there. Your posting today will be there when you are twenty years old, thirty, forty, fifty, and so on.

Surf the Internet for articles that will give you the pros and cons of social media. Read three articles, and then list five positive uses of social media and five negative uses.

Positive Uses of Social Media	Negative Uses of Social Media
1.	1.
2.	2.
3.	3.
4.	4.
5.	5.

Now think about and list one way that each of the five negative uses could become positive uses:

1.
2.
3.
4.
5.

Choose a partner, and compare and contrast your positive and negative uses. Which are similar and which are different? Compare and contrast each of your responses to how the user can make each of the five negative usages into positive usages of social media. What will you choose to do to make all your social media interactions positive?

2.9 Peer Pressure

Peer pressure is defined in the Encarta College Dictionary as "social pressure on somebody to adopt a type of behavior, dress, or attitude in order to be accepted as part of the group." Peer pressure is nothing new; nearly everyone experienced or will experience peer pressure at many points in life. The pressure seems to be particularly high, however, during the teenage years.

Your life can be permanently altered if you give in to peer pressure and use drugs and/or alcohol, engage in sex, taunt those who are defenseless, shoplift, steal cars, gang up on another girl in a verbal or physical fight—the list goes on and on. As a result of these activities, you may end up with addictions, a child, or incarcerated with a criminal record. These consequences of negative peer pressure will follow you for the rest of your life.

However, not all peer pressure is negative. Peers can exert positive pressure that can alter your life in a good way, by encouraging you to attend school every day, make good grades, participate in school activities, go to college, volunteer to help others, and set and achieve individual goals.

Search the web to find five strategies to help you to cope with and successfully manage negative peer pressure. List the success strategies below.

Strategies I Can Use to Handle Negative Peer Pressure

1.
2.
3.
4.
5.

For the next meeting of your mentoring group, interview a person you greatly respect—who is at least twenty-one years of age—about his or her experiences with peer pressure. Ask the person you interview to respond to each of the questions on the peer pressure survey.

Peer Pressure Survey

1. What is your name and age?
2. What is your occupation?
3. Describe how you saw yourself in elementary school.
4. Describe how you saw yourself in middle school.
5. Describe how you saw yourself in high school.
6. What rewards did you gain from participating in your elementary-school peer group?
7. What rewards did you gain from participating in your middle-school peer group?

8. What rewards did you gain from participating in your high-school peer group?

9. What negative outcomes did you experience in your elementary-school peer group?

10. What negative outcomes did you experience in your middle-school peer group?

11. What negative outcomes did you experience in your high-school peer group?

12. As a result of your experience, what advice do you have for me regarding peer pressure?

As a result of this interview, what did you learn about peer groups? How are the experiences of the person you interviewed similar to your experience, and how are the experiences different? What conclusions can you summarize about your interviewee's peer experiences? What did you learn about your own peer experiences? Write your responses to the questions below:

- I learned that peer groups …

- The experience of the person I interviewed was similar to my experience in the following ways:

- The experience of the person I interviewed was different from my experience in the following ways:

- I came to the following conclusions about my interviewee's experience:

- I learned the following about my peer experience by completing this activity:

Be prepared to share the results of your interview and what you learned with your mentoring group.

2.10 Is Gossip Fun?

Working in groups of two, fill out the form below:

1. What is gossip?

```



```

2. Share one or two examples of how someone spreads gossip about others. Share an additional one or two examples about how gossip was spread about you, someone in your family, or a friend. Write how it made you feel.

```



```

3. What rumors are being spread now in your school or community? How do you think those who are being gossiped about feel? Can anyone in your group talk about rumors that someone is spreading about them now? How do they feel about that gossip?

4. What are the similarities and differences in how you felt about being gossiped about and what other people felt about being gossiped about?

Similarities:

Differences:

5. Give three possible reasons why you and other people gossip.

1.

2.

3.

6. Do you want to reduce or prevent gossip? Why or why not? Brainstorm with a partner, and write down three ways to reduce or prevent gossip. If you need help, check sources on the Internet.

1.

2.

3.

Be prepared to share your responses to all questions with the group. What did you learn about yourself and gossip?

2.11 Choosing Girlfriends

Girlfriends can be a support to each other throughout life. Young women can also be *mean* to each other. They too frequently spread rumors about other young women that are not true. Because teenagers are unsure about their looks, their weight, the quality of their clothing, and their friends (both boyfriends and girlfriends), they sometimes do not think before they act. This lack of rational thinking leads to fights and suspensions from school.

The number of suspensions adds up quickly, and some young women find themselves being placed on expulsion from school. Expulsion sometimes leads to teens dropping out of school altogether, which in turn leads to other bad outcomes like teen pregnancy, alcohol and drug abuse, arrests growing out of theft to secure money to pay for drugs, and prostitution. Gang participation by teens frequently leads to court rulings that place young women in juvenile justice facilities for extended periods of time.

Along the way, the quality of the student's educational program suffers. Choosing your friends carefully and asking for adult assistance are two strategies to keep this from happening to you. List the names of up to three of your best girlfriends:

1.
2.
3.

How long have these young women been your best friends?

1.
2.
3.

List three things you would do with your girlfriends even if you knew the actions were a violation of your parents' wishes or the rules in your school (things that could get you excluded from school for five or more days):

1.
2.
3.

Why did you choose the above three actions?

Are there other options? _____ No _____ Yes
If yes, list them below:

_____

_____

_____

_____

Practice saying no to a girlfriend with a student in the group. Write your statements below after you have practiced using them.

2.12 Boyfriends: It's Your Choice

List the characteristics of the young man you would like to date. Why are these characteristics important to you?

_____

List the characteristics you will not tolerate from the young man you date.

If a young man displayed these characteristics, describe how you would break up with him:

With a partner, each take a turn role-playing this breakup so that if it comes up, you will not be afraid. Describe the feelings you experienced in your role-play:

2.13 Bullying: The Opposite of Loving Yourself

Have you ever been bullied? Have you ever bullied another girl? Access the following YouTube videos and watch them to learn more about the terrible effects of bullying:

- "SafeSchools Alert: What Is Bullying?" (http://www. youtube.com/watch?v=zUAbAKee0Cw)
- "Bullied Girl Voted the Ugliest on the Internet Gives an AMAZING Speech" (http://www.youtube.com/ watch?v=R0OV92Yyl20)
- "Cyberbully: The Saddest Part" (http://www.youtube. com/watch?v=NoRaYsbdf8M)
- "Cyberbully: Taylor Stands Up to Her Bully" (http:// www.youtube.com/watch?v=YuH9vVhDfsU)

Also, download the article about sexual orientation and bullying at http://www.stopbullying.gov/at-risk/groups/lgbt/ lgbtyouthtipsheet.pdf.

Write in the chart below what you learned from each of the videos you watched and the document you read. Be prepared to discuss your responses with your mentoring group.

"Safe Schools Alert: What Is Bullying?"	I learned …
"Bullied Girl Voted the Ugliest on the Internet Gives an AMAZING Speech"	I learned …
"Cyberbully: The Saddest Part"	I learned …

"Cyberbully: Taylor Stands Up to   I learned …
Her Bully"

Sexual-orientation document   I learned …

Explain below how your views on bullying have changed as a result of these resources.

2.14 Names Hurt

There is an old adage that states "Sticks and stone may break my bones, but words will never hurt me." What does this phrase mean to you? Do you believe this is true or false? Explain why or why not below:

Write all the words that you can think of in each of the following categories.

Category 1: Words that are encouraging, supportive, and sustaining to you and others:

Category 2: Words that are impartial, unbiased, and middle-of-the-road to you and to others:

Category 3: Words that are critical, insulting, and belittling to you and others:

Which category was most difficult for generating words? Why? Which was easiest? Why? Which do you like for people to say to you? Why? Which words will you use more of or less of in the future? Why?

It was most difficult to generate words in category ___ because:

It was easiest to generate words in category ___ because:

Of the three categories, I like for people to say words to me from category ___ because:

What I learned:

2.15 What's All This Fighting About?

Today, teenage girls who fight—in school or out of school—are all too common. Girls fight for all kinds of reasons, including the following:

- ✓ They are bullying others or being bullied themselves.
- ✓ They are jealous of another girl.
- ✓ They participate in gossip.
- ✓ They lack respect for themselves and others.
- ✓ They are trying to get attention.
- ✓ Playful bantering turns to hurtful insults.
- ✓ They are embarrassed.
- ✓ Another girl is trying to take their boyfriend.
- ✓ They are copying what they have seen on TV or in the movies.
- ✓ They think they are protecting their reputation.
- ✓ Their feelings have been hurt.
- ✓ A crowd has pushed for the fight.

You can certainly list many other reasons. However, regardless of the reason for fighting, you need to be aware that fighting is not a normal behavior. Fighting is reactionary. If you are pulled into a fight, you have given someone else control of you. You have given up your self-control and self-discipline.

Fortunately, you have the ability to make the decision *not to* fight. You have allowed your anger to take control of you, and thus you are doing and saying things that are out of your control—things you may regret later. Among the members of the animal kingdom, humans have the largest brain capacity and are the only species to have the ability to reason and think. Your great capacity for reason must be used to help you think your way out of negative situations.

Think of the possible consequences of fighting in school:

- suspension
- expulsion for an entire school year
- someone getting hurt—you or the other person might end up in the hospital or become permanently disabled
- death or prison

Fighting can result in suspension from school, which means a suspension from getting your education. It can result in an expulsion from school for an entire year, which is giving up a year of your education. Fighting can result in you or someone else being hurt to the point of being hospitalized or permanently disabled. Is fighting worth these types of consequences?

There is no way you can know how a fight will turn out until the fight is over. Therefore, the best way to be sure you have the opportunity to reach your goals and have a bright future is to think differently and make a decision to stop engaging in behavior that may get you into a fight.

Think about a situation you have either been involved in or observed that resulted in fighting. Write down the details of the incident in the box below. Also, explain how the fight ended and what the consequences were. What do you now think of those who fought?

Now surf the web, and list below three things you or the person you fought with could have done to "think" your way out of fighting.

1.
2.
3.

What will you do in the future?

Discuss with your parent(s) the ways you identified to avoid a fight. Compare your list to the advice your parent gave, and write down the ways they are similar:

Part 3

You and Your Future

This section includes the following exercises:

3.1 Think BIG: Believe, Imagine, and Grow

Determine what you think this expression means, "Think BIG: Believe, Imagine, and Grow," by reading the following selection about Congressman Emanuel Cleaver II, congressman from Kansas City, Missouri, and fill in the chart below.

5th Congressional District, MO
Congressman Emanuel Cleaver, II
Party: Democratic

Emanuel Cleaver II is now serving his fifth term representing Missouri's Fifth Congressional District, the home district of President Harry Truman.

Having served for twelve years on the city council of Missouri's largest municipality, Kansas City, Cleaver was elected as the city's first African American Mayor in 1991.

During his eight-year stint in the Office of the Mayor, Cleaver distinguished himself as an economic development activist and an unapologetic redevelopment craftsman. He and the City Council brought a number of major corporations to the city, including TransAmerica, Harley Davidson, and Citi Corp. Cleaver also led the effort, after a forty-year delay, to build the South Midtown Roadway. Upon completion of this major thoroughfare, he proposed a new name: The Bruce R. Watkins Roadway. Additionally, his municipal stewardship includes the 18th and Vine Redevelopment, a new American Royal, the establishment of a Family Division of the Municipal Court, and the reconstruction and beautification of Brush Creek.

Cleaver has received five honorary Doctoral Degrees augmented by a bachelor's degree from Prairie View

A&M of the University of Texas, and a Master's from St. Paul Theology of Kansas City.

In 2009 Cleaver was a multitude of accomplishments, both locally and congressionally, introduced the most ambitious project of his political career—the creation of a Green Impact Zone. This zone, consisting of 150 blocks of declining urban core, has received approximately $125 million dollars in American Recovery and Reinvestment funds. The Green Impact Zone is aimed at making this high-crime area the environmentally greenest piece of urban geography in the world. This project includes rebuilding Troost Avenue, rehabbing bridges, curbs and sidewalks, home weatherization, smart grid technology in hundreds of homes, and most importantly, hundreds of badly needed jobs for Green Zone residents. During the 112th Congress, Cleaver was unanimously elected the 20th chair of the Congressional Black Caucus.

Cleaver, a native of Texas, is married to the former Dianne Donaldson. They have made Kansas City home for themselves and their four children. (Source: http://cleaver.house.gov/about/full-biography)

Congressman Cleaver spoke to students at the Benjamin Banneker Charter Academy of Technology in Kansas City on Thursday, May 19, 2011. What follows is a summary of questions posed to him and the congressman's answers:

1. How did becoming the mayor affect your life?
2. What were your feelings when you endorsed Senator Clinton for president?
3. How do you feel about the troops overseas?
4. How do you feel about the price of gasoline?
5. How can our school get involved in the Green Zone?

Congressman Cleaver shared these facts about himself:

- He was born in Texas on a counter in his grandmother's kitchen.
- Segregation was harsh and cruel.
- He is one of four children of his parents; he has three sisters.
- His parents and grandparents were very poor.
- He lived in public housing until he was fourteen years of age.
- His father bought a house and had the house moved to the black area of town because of race relations.
- He could not watch TV as a child; he had to study.
- He could not use the word *lie*. The word was profane. He was raised in a strict household.
- He went to Prairie View State College, Texas (a historically black college) on a football scholarship.
- He ran track in college and had a track scholarship. Otherwise, he might not have attended college. No money!
- All his cousins, first and second, graduated from college too. He has a sister who was a school principal.
- He is proud of his work as a minister, radio talk-show host, mayor, and congressman.
- He was elected as mayor for two terms and made a significant difference.
- He has been elected to Congress for four terms (eight years).
- The Green Zone will bring Kansas City $800 billion. He gave an extended explanation about this endeavor.
- Two achievements that he is most proud of are the renovation of Brush Creek and the building of and naming of Bruce R. Watkins Highway in honor of an achieving black man.

By "thinking big" Congressman Cleaver overcame challenging circumstances.	What outcomes will you achieve by "thinking big?"

Lesson: A variety of models may be used as inspiration for you to excel.

3.2 Visualize Your Future

Goal setting requires that you ask yourself questions about your own inspiration, driving force, rationale, and reasons to really determine your goals. Those questions include:

- ✓ What do I truly enjoy doing?
- ✓ What really gets me fired up?
- ✓ What do I want to do, more than anything else?
- ✓ What settings make me feel most comfortable?
- ✓ What is my greatest desire?

No one else really knows the answers to these questions except you. You are the expert on you.

Visualize and think deeply about these questions; go beyond the first thing that comes into your mind. Write your reflective thoughts below:

✓ I truly enjoy doing …
✓ I get fired up when I …
✓ I more than anything else want to …
✓ I see myself being comfortable around …
✓ My greatest desire is to …

As a result of your responses, write a goal that will fulfill your dream. Speak aloud the words below about your goal:

- I believe I can accomplish my goal.
- I know reaching my goal will not be easy.
- I don't give up on my goal.
- I devote the amount of time needed to reach my goal.
- The rewards I receive by accomplishing my goal are worth the effort.

Now keep that mind-set, and write your goal below. Remember your goal has no limitations.

- My goal is to become _____

Complete the sentences below using the wording from the sentences above.

- I believe _____
- I know _____
- I do not _____
- I devote _____
- The rewards _____

Develop a plan to give your dream wings to fly. Sit quietly, relax, close your eyes, dream big, and visualize what you see yourself accomplishing in three months, six months, one year, and five years. Write what you visualized below. At each interval, identify the steps you will put into action to do the things you were born to do. With God, the universe, and you working together, you can't miss.

In three months, I will accomplish the following:
In six months, I will accomplish the following:
In one year, I will accomplish the following:
In two years, I will accomplish the following:
In five years, I will accomplish the following:

Lesson: Goal setting gives you crystal-clear vision on the road that is less traveled.

3.3 Superstars

Superstars come in all fields and in all sizes, shapes, and colors. The superstars below are highly educated and world renowned. They are greatly respected and have been the first African American women to reach such status in their respective fields. Use the Internet to research the educational background and accomplishments of the following superstars:

- Jackie Joyner-Kersee (http://www.biography.com/people/jackie-joyner-kersee-9358710)
- Dr. Mae Jemison (https://www.youtube.com/watch?v=EgOaIKshbIU&list=PLJT2z1tChyB0I6tBfETdI8o-1HH_eY2jK)
- First Lady Michelle Obama (https://www.youtube.com/watch?v=2Utt-6HumUU)

Choose one of these female superstars and research her educational background. Be prepared to share your findings and discuss what in your research surprised you. Reflect on and write your answer to the following question: Why do I need to continue my education? Be prepared to share your response with the mentoring group.

I need to continue my education because:

Lesson: Education levels the playing field in the game of life.

3.4 Developing Effective Habits

A habit is a behavior pattern acquired by frequent repetition. For example, many people have the habit of washing their face and then brushing their teeth before they eat breakfast or dress for work or school. Other people might have the habit of drinking a glass of water as their first task of the day. A third example is a person who gets on her knees and prays (says the Lord's prayer, turns east to Mecca, or chants) prior to beginning her routine for the day.

Habits become a way for people to focus and accomplish goals of importance to them. Some high-achieving adults attribute certain habits to their success or their failure. The following questions are designed to make you aware of how certain types of habits may contribute to successful outcomes regardless of the goals set.

1. Why do you think some people achieve their goals and others people do not? Write at least three reasons below.
2. Is it possible that a person may simply sit in silence and imagine herself being successful while completing
    ○ a single task?   Yes _____   No _____
    ○ several tasks?   Yes _____   No _____
    ○ a sequence of tasks that could lead to solving a problem? Yes _____   No _____
3. In what ways is imagining (thinking about something with one's eyes closed) a way to problem-solve in the same way that making a list is used to problem-solve?
4. Which of these strategies is superior to getting a solution to the problem?
5. Sit quietly and close your eyes. Visualize in your mind's eye every detail of what you want out of life. The greater the detail the better, because seeing is believing. Use your senses to visualize the environment, what you are wearing, what you are doing, what you hear, smell, taste, touch. Write down what you see.

My vision of my future is …

Now imagine that you have everything you wrote. Visualize your life again, but dream bigger—double it.

My second vision of my future is …

Now imagine once again that you have everything you wrote. Visualize your life again, and dream much bigger. Write it down in detail.

The third vision of my future is …

Lesson: A written plan that is reviewed and checked increases the possibility that you will achieve goals you set for yourself.

3.5 The Value of Your Education

Too often, teenagers dislike a teacher and make unwise decisions to do one or several of the following:

- skip class
- sit in the back of the class
- slouch on the desk with head down
- sleep
- doodle
- write notes
- roll eyes
- manipulate wearable technology
- find other ways to ignore or disregard what the teacher is attempting to impart to the students

Do you or anyone you know engage in this behavior?

Take a moment and think about this. Who is being punished, the teacher or the student? The teacher already has an education. The student needs to get an education.

Did you know that the level of education you obtain will directly affect the quality of your life and that of your future family? Completing high school and obtaining a high-school diploma is the minimum level of education you will need. Obtaining an associate degree will make a difference, and obtaining a bachelor's degree will make a bigger difference in the necessities, luxuries, and experiences you will be able to afford. Check out the estimates of what you will earn with different educational levels on the Bureau of Labor Statistics site at http://www.bls.gov/emp/ep_chart_001.htm.

Review and analyze the Earnings and Unemployment Rates by Educational Attainment chart. What can you conclude about the unemployment rate and the weekly income of those with less than a high-school education and those who have attained various college degrees? Report your findings below:

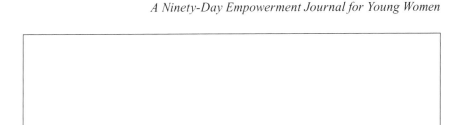

Go to http://www.bls.gov/cps/cpswom2012.pdf and review and analyze the section on Educational Attainment at the bottom of page 8 of the October 2013 Bureau of Labor Statistics "Highlights of Women's Earnings in 2012." Multiply the weekly rate of pay by fifty-two weeks per year for each education level to determine the amount per year, and then over a forty-year period of working. Report your findings for each level of education below:

Review pages 10 through 18 of this same document. Choose five professional or management occupations that you might consider in your future plans. Below, record an occupation you selected, copy the women's median weekly earnings from column 5 on the document, calculate and note what the yearly earnings would be, and then extend that to lifetime earnings using forty years of work. Repeat for each of your selected occupations.

Occupation	Women's Median Weekly Earnings	Yearly Earnings	Career Earnings
1.			
2.			
3.			
4.			
5.			

In the box below, write three paragraphs. In the first paragraph, explain the different lifestyles you are likely to have if you do the following:

- choose to graduate from high school and college
- choose to graduate from high school
- choose not to graduate from high school

In the second paragraph, explain whether you plan to drop out of high school or will stay in school regardless of whether you like or dislike all your teachers and administrators—and why. In the third paragraph, explain what your decision is about graduating from high school and going on to graduate from college, and your reasons for that decision.

Lesson: Your income may be a direct result of the type of degree you earn or the level of education you complete.

3.6 What Is Essential?

Read "Wants vs. Needs: The Secret to Successfully Prioritizing Your Expenses" on the iGrad site at http://www.igrad.com/articles/wants-versus-needs. Then surf the web to find three to five images each for "wants" and "needs."

Write your definitions of "wants" and "needs" below:

Wants	Needs

Cut out and paste the images you found into each of the categories below:

Wants	Needs

Having read the blog above, also read the Frugal Living blog post at http://frugalliving.about.com/od/bargainshopping/a/Student-Discount-Directory.htm. Feel free to search and read other blog posts or articles on wants and needs to add to your understanding.

Choose one of the occupations you listed in activity 3.5, and prepare a budget to determine how far your money will go. Watch these three videos and prepare a budget. https://www.youtube.com/watch?v=MrGWOXLtq9Y.

https://www.youtube.com/watch?v=nhBQliLydpg.

https://www.youtube.com/watch?v=_D0i_qMalQU.

Rent and utilities are at the start of the list; you complete the list of remaining items that are cited in the video clip as well as those you think are essential. Use the Internet to determine the expected costs of the items listed.

Rent:
Utilities:

Watch and take notes on videos on budgeting by Morgan Taylor (http://www.youtube.com/watch?v=WDWnLKzia78) and Not So Ordinary Wife (http://www.youtube.com/watch?v=IHnlKot5PII) to add further items to the list above or take some out. Using their advice and direction, complete your budget based on the amount of money your selected occupation will pay. Designate each item with an *N* (need) or a *W* (want). Share your list with a partner. Discuss the similarities and differences in your lists.

List below the items you will be able to afford and the items you will have to choose to give up to gain more cash on hand and in the bank.

I will be able to afford:

I will not be able to afford these items and will have to give them up:

Explain in the box below why it is important to be able to distinguish between wants and needs. Which of these two categories is most important to you today? Do you think you will choose the same category as the most important to you in five years? Why or why not? How can you afford to have more wants?

Explain below what have you learned about wants, needs, and budgeting that you can use today:

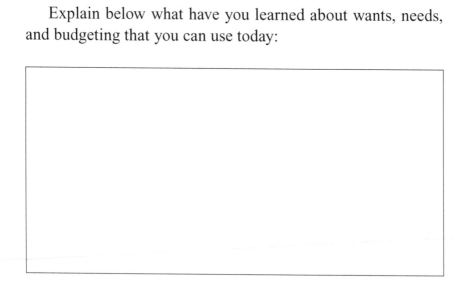

Lesson: Your wealth is a result of good spending and saving habits over a lifetime. It is comprised of small, incremental, sound financial decisions that may double, triple, or quadruple your investment.

3.7 Getting the Right Experience

When applying for a job or a volunteer assignment, you will need to first consider your future goals and what you want to become: a doctor, nurse, lawyer, teacher, business owner, journalist, actor, or other professional. Seek out those positions that will give you needed experience, help you build your skills, and give you an opportunity to experience aspects of your chosen field. For example, if you want to become a teacher, you might seek positions that allow you to interact with students of various ages and abilities. If you want to be a doctor, nurse, or other medical professional, seek experiences in a medical setting, interacting with patients and a variety of medical professionals. Other values and skills you will need for most professions are the ability to solve problems by yourself and in a group. Search the web to find specific values and skills of your chosen profession.

Experiencing work in your chosen field may reveal to you that it's not really what you had envisioned. It is extremely important that you have opportunities to find out what you will really love to do, and it is equally important to find out early what you do *not* want to do. You can learn valuable lessons from all your early positions. Also, on college applications, you can shine by having substantial work and volunteer experience to include.

Let's explore how you go about finding a part-time job or a volunteer assignment. Follow the steps below:

1. Search the web to find "typical jobs for teenagers." Select a part-time job or volunteer assignment that you want to have.
2. Search the Web to find "how to develop a teen résumé." Select guidance, and follow it to write your one-page résumé.
3. Download the sample job application for teens at http://www.afterschoolmatters.org/teens/post-secondary/sample-job-application. Complete the application as instructed.
4. Search the web for "teen job interview questions and answers."
5. Without reading the questions and answers, select a partner and determine which one of you will role-play the manager asking the questions and which will role-play the applicant and answer the questions. After the role-play, determine how closely the applicant's responses were to the answers recommended.

What did you learn about the following?

- Typical jobs and volunteer assignments for teens:

- Your résumé:

- The job application:

- Teen job-interview questions:

- Teen job-interview answers:

What else do you need to know to be ready to find your part-time job or volunteer assignment? How will you find answers to needs you identified?

Lesson: Preparation for success increases the likelihood of goal attainment.

3.8 Postsecondary Options

In today's world, more than ever, it is of the utmost importance to graduate from high school and go on to graduate from a postsecondary institution. Postsecondary institutions include four-year colleges (granting undergraduate degrees), community colleges (granting associate degrees), technical schools (granting technical certificates), or the military (granting additional training and college degrees depending on your qualifications).

It is highly recommended that you enroll in one of these postsecondary opportunities immediately after high school. Why? Because right after high school is the time when you generally have the fewest responsibilities. It is a time when most young women do not have children, husbands, or bills. Many students think they can go to work first and then go to college later. Though it can be done, many of these well-intentioned students fail to return to school after first going to work.

The time immediately following high school is most recommended for experiencing college success. It's a time when you are free to totally experience all the wonderful aspects of your next big step in education. This decision to enroll in and graduate from a postsecondary institution is guaranteed to have a positive effect on your standard of living and mental health for the rest of your life. Enrollment is your crucial step forward.

Answer the following questions about your educational plans.

1. Do you plan to attend a postsecondary option? What research have you completed concerning postsecondary options?

   a. Have you talked to someone presently enrolled in a postsecondary option?
      Yes _____ No _____
   b. Have you talked to anyone who has graduated from college?
      Yes _____ No _____
   c. Have you narrowed your postsecondary options to three?
      Yes _____ No _____

    d. What four key factors will you use to determine what postsecondary option you will pursue?
   1)
   2)
   3)
   4)

2. What makes postsecondary options special? Use prior information from friends or relatives to check all that apply. Be prepared to discuss these items in a small group.

	You meet people whose background is different from yours.
	You get to meet renowned people.
	You get to adopt new cultures, new languages, new hobbies, and new habits.
	College expands your life experience.
	You get to learn about others and yourself.
	You get a formal education.
	Education opens doors to a career. Education opens doors to graduate school, medical school, or law school.
	Education allows you to be independent.
	Through education, you learn how to think, how to process information, and how to solve problems.

Now let's do some additional research about postsecondary options. Access each of the web links listed below, which provide a wealth of information to help you. For each link, write down key information you learned that you will need to remember to enroll in the best possible postsecondary education option for you.

Mapping Your Future (http://www.mappingyourfuture.org/)

Assess Your Skills and Interest (http://www.mappingyourfuture. org/planyourcareer/skills.cfm)

Develop a Career Plan (http://www.mappingyourfuture.org/ planyourcareer/plan.cfm)

CareerShip: An Online Career Exploration Adventure (http:// www.mappingyourfuture.org/planyourcareer/careership/)

Find Work (http://www.mappingyourfuture.org/planyourcareer/findwork.cfm)

Review Other Career Resources (http://www.mappingyourfuture.org/planyourcareer/careerresources.cfm)

Choosing a School (https://studentaid.ed.gov/prepare-for-college/choosing-schools)

Applying to Schools (https://studentaid.ed.gov/prepare-for-college/applying)

Finding and Applying for Scholarships
(https://studentaid.ed.gov/types/grants-scholarships/
finding-scholarships)

Types of Aid (https://studentaid.ed.gov/types)

Forgiveness, Cancellation, and Discharge (https://studentaid.
ed.gov/repay-loans/forgiveness-cancellation)

How to Repay Your Loans (https://studentaid.ed.gov/repay-loans)

Given all the information that you have gathered and analyzed, what is your decision? Will you enroll in a postsecondary option?

Yes _____   No _____   Not Sure ___

- If yes, write your plan to enroll below.
- If no, write your plan to find a job below.
- If not sure, what additional information do you need? Write your plan to obtain this information below.

```



```

Lesson: College graduation is an attainable goal regardless of your parents' level of education or income.

3.9 Stretch Your Dollars

Oftentimes you may think you don't have enough money to get by, let alone save some of it. However, it is urgently important that you adopt the lifelong habit of saving, regardless of how much or how little money you earn. You must pay yourself first by setting aside a small percentage of your earnings every time you receive additional money. Whether the money you receive is though a part-time job, odd jobs, family or neighbors, gifts, or an allowance, always pay yourself first.

On a small scale, extra money can make a difference in whether you are able to have a single fast-food burger or a combo platter. It can make an even greater difference if your parents can't afford to send you to college. You can get loans to go to college, but you will need money from your savings to participate in recreational and other entertainment activities that are very much a part of the college lifestyle. A little savings each time you receive money will add up to a lot over time. The more savings you have, the more choices you can make.

Access the website at http://www.themint.org/teens/saving-tricks.html and read "Savings Tricks" and "Tricks Our Minds Play with Money," and then take "The Truth About Millionaires Quiz."

1. What is saving money about?

2. Why is consistency important when you are saving money?

3. Name three things you really want and would be willing to save to get.

4. What would you be willing to sacrifice now in order to buy those items listed in #3?

5. What type of income do you receive or earn? What is the total dollar amount of this income? How much will you pledge to save each time you receive income? How much will you have saved in one year, two years, and three years?

6. What did you learn from "The Truth About Millionaires Quiz" about savings?

```
┌─────────────────────────────────────────────┐
│                                               │
│                                               │
│                                               │
│                                               │
│                                               │
│                                               │
└─────────────────────────────────────────────┘
```

With your parent or guardian, open a savings account and make your first deposit. Be prepared to discuss the "opening a savings account" experience. What did you think, feel, see, and touch? On a scale of 1 to 5 (1 = terrible, 5 = excellent), rate your experience. Explain why you gave the experience that rating.

Lesson: Wealth is the result of good spending and saving habits over a lifetime. Wealth is comprised of small, incremental, researched financial decisions that may double, triple, or quadruple your investments.

3.10 Obstacles to Overcome

There always will be obstacles that get in the way of your plans. Some will be large, and some will be small. What becomes important is how well you remain focused on what you want to achieve.

Think about a recent decision you made with a friend that resulted in a difficult conversation with your parent or another adult over why you did what you did. List a couple of things you could have done differently to avoid that conversation. For example:

Incident

Homework was not completed and submitted to the teacher on time because I spent all my study time talking on the phone with my friend.

Alternatives

- Rather than call my friend and talk for three hours, I will establish a regular schedule for completing my homework and follow the schedule.
- I will identify a study buddy and contact her when I experience a problem answering a difficult question in my homework.

Now describe an incident or obstacle:

List two alternatives you could use to keep the incident or obstacles listed above from getting in your way again:

1.

2.

Lesson: Think decisions through before implementing them. Write steps you can follow to overcome obstacles. This will help tremendously with your future decisions.

3.11 Unhealthy Habits

Smoking

Do you smoke? Yes _____ No _____
How old were you when you started smoking? _____
Do your parents or other relatives smoke? Yes _____ No _____
Do you have friends who smoke? Yes _____ No _____
View this YouTube video on the negative effects of smoking:
http://www.youtube.com/watch?v=l26f4f-V4jc.

List three negative effects of smoking that you didn't previously know:

1. _____
2. _____
3. _____

Drinking

View this video on the effects of alcohol abuse: http://www.youtube.com/watch?v=33Lp0CIgOGs.

List three negatives of alcohol abuse that you learned from the video:

1. _____
2. _____
3. _____

View a website designed especially to help African American women become healthy. A healthy lifestyle will help you to maximize your thinking, believing, imagining, and growing.

Choose an article on the website on a topic of interest to you. Write a summary of the article to share with your mentoring group. The end result of this sharing will be increased knowledge of how to become a healthy woman. Also, while you are on the site, sign up to receive newsletters on African American women's health.

Lesson: Decide as a class what lessons you learned from the vast amount of information you gleaned from the websites you visited.

3.12 Images of Young Women

Generally, there are systemic, structural, and institutional challenges that girls—black, white, Hispanic, Jewish, Polish, Indian, Arabic, Asian—face. However, African American girls' challenges are especially dramatic: 37 percent of black girls grow up in poverty, and 57 percent of them live in single-parent homes, which means they have access to fewer social and economic resources than other girls. Many attend underfunded schools. They also suffer under the assault of negative media depictions; racial profiling enforced by security guards, teachers, and surveillance cameras; and the excessive discipline that impacts black boys, their brothers.

Here is a list of stereotyped depictions of African American females in media, such as music videos, reality TV shows, and YouTube; in ads on billboards and in magazines; and on advertisements on public transportation:

- caretaking "mammies"
- sexually promiscuous "Jezebels" and "Sapphires"
- sex freaks
- materialistic "gold diggers"
- high-maintenance "divas"
- violent "gangster bitches"

These images fit the stereotypes created about black females: trashy, ghetto, loud, disrespectful, and disruptive.

Brainstorm five four-letter words that are positive and refute these negative stereotypes. Share with a partner your four-letter words that affirm your strengths and hopes for the future.

How does using these positive words make you feel compared to the use of negative four-letter words? In what settings can you use these positive four-letter words more and negative words less?

Say these words aloud:

- "I am magnificent, and my greatness is real."
- "If I can believe it, I can achieve it."

Give two examples of when you have believed something and it was achieved.

Now write five steps you will take in daily living to ensure that none of the stereotypes will describe you.

Step One	
Step Two	
Step Three	
Step Four	
Step Five	

Lesson: Behave in ways that do not reinforce stereotypes.

3.13 Affirmations for Your Future

According to Louise Hay, an affirmation is a beginning point on the path to change. In essence, a person is saying to her subconscious mind the following: "I am taking responsibility. I am aware that there is something I can do to change." A person consciously chooses words that will either help eliminate something from her life or help create something new in her life.

Doing, thinking, or writing an affirmation is consciously choosing to think certain thoughts that will manifest positive results in the future. Affirmations create a focal point that will allow you to start changing your thinking. Affirmative statements go beyond the reality of the present into the creation of the future through the words you use in the now.

It is important for you to always say your affirmations in the present tense and without contractions. For example, typical affirmations would start with "I have" or "I am." If you write or say, "I am going to" or "I will have," your thoughts stay out there in the future. The universe always takes your thoughts and words literally and gives you what you say you want.

As Louise Hay writes in her book *Experience Your Good Now! Learning to Use Affirmation*, "Every thought you think counts, so don't waste your precious thoughts. Every positive thought brings good into your life. Every negative thought pushes good away; it keeps it just out of your reach." It is moreover, imperative, according to Hay, that you "don't blame others for what is seemingly wrong in your life—that's just another waste of time. Remember—you're under the laws of your own consciousness, your own thoughts, and you attract specific experiences to you as a result of the way you think."

Daily Relationship Affirmations

Make the following affirmations a part of your daily routine. Say them often while looking in the mirror, or any time you feel your negative beliefs surfacing. It is most appropriate for you to say them on the way to school daily (on the bus, in the car, or while walking to school). You might also keep a diary and write each sentence at least fifteen times daily:

- I am willing to release any pattern within me that creates troubled friendships.
- My friends are loving and supportive.
- As I release all criticism, judgmental people leave my life.
- It is safe for me to ask for what I want.
- I respect others, and they respect me.
- My love and acceptance of others creates lasting friendships.
- I am open and receptive to all points of view.

Post the following friendship affirmation in your bedroom or in a place of your choice where you may view it daily, sometimes more than once. The messages in the affirmation will transform your self-esteem and relationships with your family, relatives, and friends.

Friendship Treatment
by Louise Hay

(from the *You Can Heal Your Life
Affirmation Kit Guidebook,*
Hay House, Inc., Carlsbad, California, 2005, p. 84)

I am one with Life, and all of Life loves and supports
me. Therefore, I claim for myself a joyous, loving circle
of friends. We all have such good times individually
and together. I am not my parents or their relationships.
I am my own unique self, and I choose to only allow
supportive, nurturing people in my world. Wherever I
go I am greeted with warmth and friendliness. I deserve
the best friends, and I allow my life to be filled with love
and joy. This is the truth of my being, and I accept it as
so. All is well in my friendly world.

Lesson: You are under the laws of your own consciousness.
You attract specific experiences as a result of the way you think.

Mantras

Earlier, you were introduced to affirmations and the power
they have if you use them as a part of your daily living. This
is also true for your practice of visualization. A third word
that compels users to be introspective is the practice of using
mantras. A mantra is:

1. A holy word in meditation: in Hindu and Buddhist
   religious practice, a sacred word, chant, or sound that is
   repeated during meditation to facilitate spiritual power
   and transformation of consciousness.

2. An expression or idea that is repeated, often without thinking about it, and closely associated with something.

Synonyms for *mantra* include chant, intonation, repetition, refrain, sacred word, hymn, song, and word.

Mantras, affirmations, and positive visualization are powerful intellectual tools. Use that power. Here is a meditation list you may use:

- I see only harmony around me at all times. I am always safe and secure.
- I accept life as safe and joyous. Only good comes to me and through me.
- Today is a wonderful day. I choose to make it so.
- I deserve the best, and I accept it now. All my needs and desires are met before I even ask.
- I am willing to learn to love myself.
- Others are different, not wrong. We are all one.
- I am at home in my body.

Write three of these on a sheet of paper and tape them on your mirror to remind you of these promises that you have made to yourself.

Which three did you choose? Why did you choose them? Be prepared to discuss with a peer.

1. I chose _____

   because _____

   _____

2. I chose _____

   because _____

   _____

3. I chose _____

    because _____

    _____

These mantras and affirmations will come true. When you see evidence of these promises to yourself, record the event and the positive experience it brought you.

The Event	Positive Experience It Brought

Lesson: The use of mantra will calm you, energize you, and enable you to be more receptive and thoughtful when interacting with others.

3.14 An Attitude of Gratitude

Many of you have heard positive phrases that are said over and over to you by your parents, grandparents or others, such as, "If you don't succeed, try, try again." Have you ever thought about the deeper meaning of this phrase? The deeper meaning is to *never* give up on your dreams. Think it through, devise a plan, and try another more successful way to achieve them.

Below, write a positive phrase that you've heard and explain the deeper meaning you find in this phrase.

The phrase:

The deeper meaning:

Share these phrases and the deeper meanings aloud in your group.

Write the name of the person whose phrase and deeper meaning you wrote in the box above. Write a note of gratitude to this person for loving and supporting you.

Decide how and when you will share your gratitude with this person—for example, call, text, Facebook, or other method. How does expressing gratitude make you feel? Plan to report back to the group the person's response to your expression of gratitude.

Lesson: Gratitude is giving and receiving. Open your heart every day to new people and new experiences that affirm you and motivate you to give more of yourself to others.

3.15 Rites of Passage

You have finished the first portion of a wonderful journey into yourself. However, this is really just the beginning of your lifelong effort to be all you were intended to be. As part of the final activities, we encourage you to become familiar with the Seven Principles of Nguzo Saba.

In 1966, civil-rights leader Maulana Ron Karenga conceived the idea of a special holiday geared specifically to the African American community. Karenga created a seven-day celebration that embraces African Americans' heritage and a sense of human values. All seven of the principles are worthy of deep reflection.

View a video on the origin of Kwanzaa and black history at http://www.history.com/topics/holidays/kwanzaa-history/videos/origins-of-black-history-month. Download and read "The RBG Kwanzaa (Nguzo Saba) Booklet" from http://www.slideshare.net/rbgstreetscholar1/the-rbg-kwanzaa-nguzo-saba-booklet-for-downloadwith-mp3s-included. Finally, listen to some of the free downloadable Kwanzaa music at http://www.theholidayspot.com/kwanzaa/kwanzaa_music.htm.

Review and discuss the significance of Black History Month and the seven-day celebration of Kwanzaa. Explain how they are similar and how they are different. Explain how and why they are needed.

Adapt this seven-day celebration into a onetime ceremony and celebration highlighting each of the seven Kwanzaa principles. Each member of the mentoring group is to choose a role to play in the presentation, including preparing the table, making the food, lighting a candle, writing an example of how the mentoring group has embraced the meaning of each concept, and speaking during the ceremony.

The purpose of this book is to ensure that every teen and young adult female is able to define herself, name herself, and speak for herself instead of being defined and spoken for by others. This affirmation is the principle of self-determination—*kujichagulia*—and it's one that every member of the mentoring group needs to deeply embrace. Each young woman is to prepare a one- to three-minute speech to share during the ceremony about how this mentoring process has increased her self-determination and what she will do next to ensure that she keeps and increases her self-determination.

Finally, at the ceremony, each young woman will identify a younger female to mentor (this mentee has to want and agree to be mentored). At the ceremony, each mentoring member will share the mentee's name, age, why she chose this mentee, when they will meet, and what they will do at their first mentoring encounter.

Enjoy the rest of the journey, and meet every situation with confidence.

Lesson: Stay grateful, motivated, strong, and determined to reach your loftiest goals.

Resources

Internet Sites

Throughout this journal, users are encouraged to access the Internet to obtain important information to complete learning experiences. The following are additional resources that may be of use:

- "How to Use Affirmations Effectively," *Wikihow*, http://www.wikihow.com/Use-Affirmations-Effectively #Deciding on the Content of Your Affirmations.
- "The Only 100 Positive Affirmations You Will Ever Need," *Prolific Living*, http://www.prolificliving. com/100-positive-affirmations/.
- "Positive Affirmations for Teens" Flashcards, Quizlet, https://quizlet.com/10743789/positive-affirmations-for-teens-flash-cards/.
- United Negro College Fund, www.uncf.org.

Magazines

- *Ebony*, http://www.ebony.com.
- *Essence*, http://www.essence.com.

Books

Angelou, Maya. *Now Sheba Sings the Song*. New York: E. P. Dutton/Dial Books, 1987 (a book illustrated by Tom Feelings and appropriate for reading aloud to a group or a larger audience).

Breathnach, Sarah Ban. *Simple Abundance: A Daybook of Comfort and Joy*. New York: Warner Books, Inc., 1995.

———. *The Simple Abundance Journal of Gratitude*. New York: Warner Books, Inc., 1996.

Cook, Suzan D. Johnson. *Sister to Sister Devotions, for and from African American Women*. Valley Forge, PA: Judson Press, 1995.

Covey, Sean. *The 7 Habits of Highly Effective Teens*. New York: Simon & Schuster, 1998.

Davis, Darren G. *Female Force: Condoleezza Rice*. Blue Water Comics, April 2009, http://www.bluewaterprod.com.

———. *Female Force: Michelle Obama*. Blue Water Comics, April 2009, http://www.bluewaterprod.com.

Davis, Sampson, George Jenkins, and Rameck Hunt. *The Pact*. New York: Riverhead Books, 2002.

Edelman, Marian Wright. *Lanterns: A Memoir of Mentors*. Boston: Beacon Press, 1999.

Edwards, Robert. *Who Is Barack Obama?* New York: Grosset & Dunlap, 2009.

Galens, Judy. *Queen Latifah*. People in the News Series. Farmington Hills, MI: Lucent Books, 2007.

Grimes, Nikki. *Barack Obama, Son of Promise, Child of Hope*. New York: Simon & Schuster Books for Young Readers,

2008 (a book illustrated by Bryan Collier and appropriate for reading aloud to a group or a large audience).

Harper, Hill. *Letters to a Young Brother*. New York: Gotham, 2006.

———. *Letters to a Young Sister*. New York: Gotham, 2008.

Hay, Louise L. *You Can Heal Your Life*. Carlsbad, CA: Hay House, Inc., 2004.

Hunter, Latoya. *The Diary of Latoya Hunter*. New York: Vintage Books, 1993.

Jasen, Julie. *I Don't Know What I Want, but I Know It's Not This*. New York: Penguin Group, 2003.

Obama, Barack. *The Audacity of Hope: Thoughts on Reclaiming the American Dream*. New York: Crown Publishers, 2006.

———. *Of Thee I Sing: A Letter to My Daughters*. New York: Alfred A. Knopf, 2010 (a book illustrated by Loren Long and appropriate for reading aloud to a group or a larger audience).

Payment, Simone. *Queen Latifah*. The Library of Hip-Hop Biographies. New York: the Rosen Publishing Group, Inc., 2006.

Schlink, Bernard. *The Reader*. New York: Vintage International, 1995.

Simone, Nina, with Stephen Cleary. *I Put a Spell on You*. New York: Pantheon Books, 1991.

Snyder, Gail. *Hip Hop Queen Latifah*. Broomall, PA: Mason Crest Publishers, 2007.

Thomas, Pat. *The Skin I'm In*: *A First Look at Racism*. Illustrated by Lesley Harper. Hauppauge, NY: Barron's Educational Series, Inc., 2003.

Todd, C. Angela, and C. Ann Todd. *Watch Out for the Elephants*. Leawood, KS: Leathers Publishing, 2004.

Urban, Hal. *Life's Greatest Lessons*: *20 Things That Matter*. 4th ed. New York: Simon & Schuster, 2003.

Zadra, Dan. *Gratitude*. Seattle, WA: Compendium Publishing, 2005.

Bibliography

Birchett, Colleen, Tiauna Boyd, Iva E. Carruthers, and Alison Gise Johnson. *The New Jim Crow Study Guide*. Chicago: the Samuel DeWitt Proctor Conference, Inc., 2011.

Cook, Suzan D. Johnson. *Sister to Sister Devotions, for and from African American Women*. Valley Forge, Judson Press, 1995.

Covey, Sean. *The Seven Habits of Highly Effective Teens*. New York: Fireside, 1998.

Edelman, Marian Wright. *The Measure of Our Success*. Boston: Beacon Press, 1992.

Gawain, Shakti. *Creative Visualization*. Novato, CA: New World Library Publishing, 1985.

Gray, John. *Men Are from Mars, Women Are from Venus*. New York: HarperCollins Publishers, Inc., 1992.

Harper, Hill. *Letters to a Young Brother*. New York: Gotham, 2006.

———. *Letters to a Young Sister*. New York: Gotham, 2008.

Hay, Louise L. *Meditations to Heal Your Life*. Carlsbad: Hay House, Inc., 2006.

————. *You Can Heal Your Life*. Carlsbad, CA: Hay House, Inc., 2005.

Jasen, Julie. *I Don't Know What I Want, But I Know It's Not This*. New York: Penguin Group, 2003.

Johnson, Spence. *Who Moved My Cheese? for Teens*. New York: G. P. Putman's Sons, 2002.

Miller, D. Patrick. *A Little Book of Forgiveness*. New York: Viking, 1994.

Ryan, M. J. *Attitudes of Gratitude*: *How to Give and Receive Joy Every Day of Your Life*. New York: MJF Books, 1999.

Thondup, Tulku. *The Healing Power of Mind: Simple Meditation Exercises for Health, Well-Being, and Enlightenment*. Boston: Shambala, 1996.

Todd, C. Angela, and C. Ann Todd. *Watch Out for the Elephants*. Leawood, KS: Leathers Publishing, 2004.

Urban, Hal. *Life's Greatest Lessons: 20 Things That Matter*. 4th ed. New York: Simon & Schuster, 2003.

Wellington, Sheila, and Catalyst. *Be Your Own Mentor*. New York: Random House, 2001.

Printed in the United States
By Bookmasters